Thorne Moors

also by Catherine Caufield

*The Emperor of the United States and
other Magnificent British Eccentrics
In the Rainforest
Multiple Exposures*

Catherine Caufield

is a writer who now lives in San Francisco.
Her work has appeared in
*New Scientist, International Herald Tribune,
The Guardian* and *New Statesman.*
She is a regular contributor to
The New Yorker

Fay Godwin

has published thirteen books including
Land and *Our Forbidden Land*
She was the 1987 Fellow at the National Museum
of Photography, Film & Television,
Bradford
and in 1990 received an honorary Fellowship
from the Royal Photographic Society
in Bath.

Catherine Caufield

THORNE MOORS

with a photographic essay by
Fay Godwin

The Sumach Press

first published in Great Britain by
The Sumach Press
29 Mount Pleasant, St. Albans, Herts AL3 4QY

the text first appeared in
The New Yorker, February 1991

British Library Cataloguing in Publcation Data
Caufield, Catherine
Thorne Moors.
1. Title
333.7809425

ISBN 0-7126-5166-7 hbk
ISBN 0-7126-5167-5 pbk

designed by
Ken Garland and Associates

typeset by SX Composing Ltd, Rayleigh, Essex

plates printed in Great Britain by
Jackson Wilson Ltd, Leeds
bound by Mackays of Chatham

I am grateful to the many people
who generously helped me to learn about Thorne Moors.
In particular I owe thanks to
Brian Eversham, Jane Smart of Plantlife, Phil Williams,
and the wonderful people at the Doncaster Museum,
especially Colin Howes and Peter Skidmore.
I would also like to salute 'Betty' Bunting
for keeping up with the remarkable man she married
more than half a century ago.

contents

William Bunting

to
William Bunting
Naturalist, Pamphleteer, Archivist, Rebel,
Bad-tempered old sod,
and Inspiration

Gringley Beacon, an ancient lookout site two hundred and fifty feet above sea level, is the highest point on the Humberhead Levels – a vast plain at the head of the Humber estuary that is the traditional boundary between Yorkshire and Lincolnshire. From that modest rise, on a crisp June morning, I could see the spire of York Minster, forty miles to the north, and also that of Lincoln Cathedral, twenty miles to the southeast. More interesting to me, however, was the near landscape – a patchwork of hedgerow-bound fields, some yellow with the flowers of oilseed rape, some green with ripening grain, some the rich brown of ploughed-up soil. Superimposed on the landscape are villages linked by thin ribbons of road, isolated red brick and red-tile-roofed cottages and farm buildings, and here and there a small wood.

Wetlands once extended in every direction from this point, but now their only sizeable remnant is Thorne Moors, to the north, a rough, uncultivated area in the middle distance. Virtually all the rest of the land has been drained, embanked and turned into farmland, the excess water channelled into a complex system of crisscrossing drains, ditches and canals that cut across the countryside – not with the curves and bends of natural watercourses but with the straight lines and right angles of the drawing board. Yet, standing there, one can imagine the landscape as it was thousands of years ago, and as it largely remained until the last few centuries: a patchwork of lakes, peat bogs, marshes, and swamps, punctuated by a few gentle rises – islands of drier land, where villages and farms were concentrated.

Wetlands such as Thorne Moors are generally regarded – when they are regarded at all – as wastelands, uninteresting and unattractive. It is true that wetlands have little to offer those who are used to admiring landscapes through the window of a car going fifty miles an hour, but they do have their passionate admirers. 'Any fool can appreciate mountain scenery, but it takes a man of discernment to appreciate the fens,' a resident of the Cambridge fenlands once remarked to the British botanist Sir Harry Godwin. The very flatness and featurelessness that make wetlands uninteresting to the hurried passer-by give some observers the sense of being in a limitless wilderness. One's view to the horizon is unblocked by trees, buildings or mountains; the land stretches away, apparently to infinity. In these unprettied places, one feels entirely free of the works of man. They impart feelings of desolation, of emptiness, of peace.

Thorne Moors is such a place. Though it is so close to the city of York, it conveys a sense of isolation and wildness. People call the area 'godforsaken' – and in today's crowded Britain they mean that as a compliment.

There are no buildings on Thorne Moors, and the only landmarks are the towers of a colliery on its western edge and the steeple of Goole Church, five miles from its northern edge. But the hand of man has been at work on the moors for more than three millennia, draining the land, digging canals, cutting peat and using river silt to create farmland. This human interference has actually increased the variety of habitats on what remains of the moorland. The old peat diggings, disused canals, abandoned fields, wet pasture, open waterways and other habitats enable Thorne Moors to support an immense variety of wildlife.

More than four thousand species of plants and animals, including more than twenty-five of Britain's rarest and most severely endangered species, live on Thorne Moors. It is especially rich in insect life, and is the one place in Britain where the mire pill beetle lives. Until the nineteen-seventies, that insect was known to exist only in southern Bavaria and around the Baltic Sea; then, in 1972, archaeologists working on Thorne Moors turned up a fossilized specimen three thousand years old, and five years later a living mire pill beetle was discovered on the moorland. Since then, several colonies of them have been found. Thorne Moors is also the only place in northern England where a rare arachnid appears – the three-inch-long giant raft spider. Almost two hundred species of birds feed or breed on Thorne Moors. Seventy-five species nest there, including the nightjar, a rare and elusive bird with a haunting evening song; some forty pairs of nightjars now breed on the moors. Wild cranberries, southern marsh orchids, and the insect-eating bladderwort grow there. One reason for Thorne's unusually high diversity of species is that it straddles an invisible line running across Britain from east to west and dividing the island into two biological regions. It is thus home to many species that ordinarily do not mix. Southern species such as the nightingale, the reed damsel-bug, and the marsh pea coexist there with northern species like the heather linnet, the large heath butterfly, and the increasingly rare bog rosemary.

The landscape that provides this diversity was born during the last ice age. About eighteen thousand years ago, a glacier blocked the Humber Gap, a pass between the Yorkshire and the Lincolnshire hills through which inland rivers flowed into the Humber estuary and, ultimately, to the North Sea. The trapped river water formed a huge lake at the head of the estuary. Seven thousand years later, with the ice receding, the lake bed had become a vast sediment-filled plain – the Humberhead Levels.

Five thousand years ago, much of the Humberhead Levels, including Thorne Moors, was covered with a dense forest dominated by linden trees and containing many other broadleaf species, among them oak, hazel and ash. Despite some clearing for agriculture and settlements, the forest thrived for several thousand years. Then, quite suddenly, it disappeared, and was supplanted by marshes and peat bogs. The speculation until recently was that the forest had been overcut by Neolithic farmers or had been deliberately destroyed by the Romans in order to deprive the Brigantes and other rebellious tribes of a base for guerrilla warfare, but twentieth-century pollen studies show that nature, not man, destroyed the forest. More than three thousand years ago, rising sea levels, caused by melting ice-fields, pushed the Humber estuary farther inland, making rivers back up and overflow into the forest. The waterlogged soil choked and killed the trees.

Over most of the Humberhead Levels, the forest was transformed into reed swamp, dotted here and there with lakes and with drier, wooded areas, and marked by a tracery of meandering rivers, but at Thorne Moors and a few other places evolution took a different course. These areas were extremely poor in nutrients, and while most plants cannot tolerate such soil a few specialized plants require nutrient-poor, acidic conditions. Perhaps the best-adapted ones are the sphagnum mosses, which are virtual machines for absorbing water and nutrients. Sphagnum mosses are so efficient at capturing and holding whatever water falls on them that they create a waterlogged, airless environment devoid of the bacteria, worms and insects that promote decomposition. When the mosses die, therefore, they do not decay; instead, layers of dead organic matter accumulate, forming peat. The low nutrient levels on Thorne Moors and the resultant colonization by sphagnum moss transformed the moors into an unusual type of wetland – a raised peat bog. While this type of habitat was once widespread in Britain, ninety-six per cent of Britain's raised peat bogs have now been destroyed, according to government figures, and Thorne Moors, which takes in forty-seven hundred acres, is currently the country's largest example of such habitat. In the words of a South Yorkshire County Council internal memorandum written in 1979, Thorne Moors is 'an ecological gem, a site that . . . remains one of the Nation's most important natural history areas'. The Government has since named Thorne Moors one of the country's most important nature-conservation sites.

Some raised bogs have been known to stand thirty feet or more above the surrounding countryside, always maintaining their waterlogged condition, thanks to the sphagnum mosses. They lie on the landscape like huge raindrops, in apparent defiance of the laws of gravity. An undisturbed raised bog may be as much as ninety-eight per cent water. However, its domed shape makes it especially vulnerable to water loss; drainage from any part of the bog may damage the whole, causing many species of plants and animals to disappear as the peat dries out. By the mid-eighteenth century, Thorne Moors had formed some twenty feet of peat, and was so liquid that it was called a quaking bog. One nineteenth-century naturalist, Adrian Woodruffe-Peacock, a Lincolnshire vicar, described it as 'trembling in waves when you jumped on its . . . surface, till the undulations were lost in the distance or at the edge of the nearest ditch'.

He went on to say, 'No man could traverse these water cuts . . . without "fen boards", for less than five minutes would have sunk the strongest swimmer overhead in black, oozy peat about eleven feet deep' – fen boards being somewhat like short, fat, skis. Thorne Moors was most tremulous in the winter, when its mosses absorbed large amounts of rainwater. Woodruffe-Peacock wrote that Thorne Moors stood six or eight feet taller in the winter than in the summer.

Because the waterlogged soil of a peat bog preserves not only the plants and the animals that grow in it but also anything that falls into it, peat bogs are one of our best records of the ancient past. On Thorne Moors, the peat grew up so quickly – within five hundred years, more than three feet of peat had formed – that the fallen trees of the forest it displaced had become embedded in the protective peat before they had a chance to decay. There are no primeval woodlands left standing in Britain, so the fallen but preserved trees of Thorne Forest are among the few records of the lost ancient forests of Western Europe.

So well preserved is this forest that it is almost impossible to distinguish a three-thousand-year-old branch from a recently fallen one. During a walk on the moors last summer, I picked up a pine branch that had been dislodged by a bulldozer working in the area. Where it had broken from the tree I could count the annual rings; the bark was intact but slightly dark, from the tannic acid in the bog water. It looked more like part of a living tree than any piece of driftwood I'd ever found, and its great age didn't really register with me until, on the way home, I told the woman who runs the only Chinese restaurant in the village of Thorne about it. She took it gently in her hands and gazed at it for a long moment, softly repeating the phrase, 'Three thousand years old.'

Many things besides trees are buried in the peat of Thorne Moors. Pollen grains from neighbouring areas were blown on to the bog over the centuries, giving us a record of local trade, agriculture, flora and fauna and climate which dates back to Neolithic times. Such records are crucial to our understanding of prehistoric societies, plant and insect evolution, and long-term climatic change. Though Thorne Moors' peat record has not been systematically studied, nearby have yielded valuable information, including most of what we know about early boats and boating in northwestern Europe. The oldest plank boats in the world outside Egypt were found in peat deposits at North Ferriby, only twenty miles northeast of Thorne; their age is estimated at nearly three thousand years. Chance finds around Thorne in earlier centuries include a fine jadeite axe of Eastern European origin, and a collar of twisted gold from Ireland. In the late seventeenth century, Abraham de la Pryme, the curate of Hatfield and later the vicar of Thorne, mentioned in his diary the discovery in the Thorne peat some years earlier of a perfectly preserved man 'laying at his length, with his head upon his arm, as in a common posture of sleep'. In 1971, archaeologists unearthed a rare Bronze Age wooden pathway, which local people apparently laid through Thorne Forest about three thousand years ago, when water levels were rising and the ground was becoming too boggy to walk on.

Despite its beauty, its rarity, and its biological wealth, the three-thousand-year-old Thorne Moors is today on the verge of extinction. Visitors who approach the moorland from its western border see the vast wetland wilderness stretching to the horizon, but those who come in from the east, along a newly built road that penetrates to the heart of the moors, see a very different scene – hundreds of acres of barren ground devoid of all vegetation. From the first prospect, one looks out on the results of ten thousand years of evolution, thousands of years of human history, centuries of human use, and decades of preservation battles. From the second prospect, one sees the effects of less than five years of intensive peat extraction. Virtually all of the land is owned by Fisons, a multinational company based in Ipswich, and if Fisons has its way almost the entire area will have been scraped bare within twenty years, its peaty soil dug up and sold to gardeners for use as potting compost, soil conditioner and mulch.

From the days of William the Conqueror until three or four centuries ago, much of the southern half of the Humberhead Levels - some two hundred and seventy square miles – formed a huge royal hunting estate known as Hatfield Chase, which encompassed Thorne Moors and much other land. It was the largest game preserve in England, according to Vernon Cory, the author of 'Hatfield and Axholme: An Historical Review'. Such royal hunting grounds were not uninhabited, nor were they owned exclusively by the Crown. Thousands of people lived within the Chase, and there were many private landholdings that pre-dated the area's designation as a royal estate. In the fifteenth century, the Chase and its surroundings were placed under the rule of 'forest law', which forbade anyone to interfere with deer or other huntable animals, such as boars, swans and otters, even if the animals damaged crops on private land. But Hatfield Chase had no resident lord of the manor, so the forest law was not strictly enforced. Dan Byford, a historian who specializes in the agriculture of Hatfield Chase, says that that laxity attracted many poor people to the Chase, where they could fish and trap relatively undisturbed and might hope to find some unused land to work.

Agriculture in and around the Chase was largely pastoral, although even the dry areas were regularly flooded. Pastures were under water from November to April; in the spring, the river waters receded, leaving behind a layer of rich silt; in the summer and the autumn, animals were turned out to graze on these naturally fertilized fields. Over the centuries, sporadic efforts were made to extend and intensify agriculture by improving land drainage, but technical limitations and the fact that local people depended upon the fish and game of the wetlands moderated the degree of change.

Until the seventeenth century, Hatfield Chase remained a great wetland wilderness – a mosaic of water meadows, peat bogs, reed beds, rivers, lakes, woods and small settlements. Wetlands such as these were places apart; they were ignored, and even feared, by the rest of the world. Outsiders were intimidated by their boggy vastness and by their winter floods, which could isolate a village or a hamlet for months at a time. The waterlogged soil would not support roads, and walking across the moors was dangerous: a man could easily lose his way in the flat, featureless landscape, and one wrong step into a quaking bog could cost him his life. One early-nineteenth-century writer noted, 'So wild a country nurses up a race of people as wild.' These 'wild' people, the wetlands villagers, developed a unique way of life and an independent cast of mind. They were equally at home navigating the marshes in boats and on stilts. They roamed freely over hundreds of square miles of land rich in deer, otters, salmon, herons, swans and ducks. They could hunt and fish, graze cattle, gather cranberries and dig peat for fuel, and make a good living doing so.

In 1690, Hatfield Chase received a rare royal visit. Prince Henry, the elder son of James I, came to hunt, and to consider the future of the Chase. For the hunt, five hundred deer were driven into Thorne Mere, a large lake near Thorne, where scores of hunters in boats awaited them with clubs and spears. The event was recorded in an oil painting by an unknown artist of the day. He depicts an idyllic scene – a peaceful lake, a dramatic sky, and laughing hunters and boatmen – but what appears to be a patch of floating vegetation in the middle of the lake is actually the antlers of a herd of panicked deer huddling together as their water-borne stalkers approach. With the royal party were two men who symbolized the conflict into which the area was soon to be plunged – Robert Portington, a local landowner, and an engineer, said to be Cornelius Vermuyden, scion of a Dutch drainage dynasty.

The Dutch were the acknowledged masters of land drainage in Europe at that time, turning more than four thousand acres of marshland and mud flats into productive farmland every year. Prince Henry, an enthusiastic advocate of land drainage, used the hunt as an opportunity to get an expert opinion on the feasibility of draining the Chase. Henry died three years later, before he was able to put any of his plans into action. In 1625, his younger brother succeeded to the throne as Charles I. In need of money for his war with Spain (a war that Parliament refused to finance), Charles signed a contract with Vermuyden for the drainage of sixty thousand acres of Hatfield Chase and parts of a neighbouring area called the Isle of Axholme. Under the agreement, Vermuyden and his financial backers would receive a third of the newly drained land, the King would retain a third, and the commoners would receive the remaining third. (In law, commoners are those who have rights over a piece of land that someone else owns. Such rights – to graze animals, collect firewood or cut peat, for example – ordinarily belong to those who live in certain houses or cottages in the district.) This was the first major drainage scheme – and the first great civil-engineering project – in English history.

Vermuyden found fifty-seven 'Participants', or investors, almost all of them Dutch, to finance his plan, and he imported a crew of his fellow-countrymen to do the work, which consisted mainly of cutting huge drains and ditches across the countryside. The Participants, who had been looking forward to owning large areas of productive English farmland, soon discovered that their investment was anything but a safe one. The main technical problem Vermuyden faced in trying to improve the drainage of the low-lying site was that the Ouse and the Trent, the rivers that carried the area's water out to sea, were both tidal for considerable stretches. This meant that twice each day the water level in the Trent and the Ouse was so high that discharges from their tributary rivers – the Don, the Idle, and the Torne – were impeded. Vermuyden put forward a sweeping plan, which involved diverting all three of the rivers that flowed through the Chase so that they could discharge continuously, as well as building numerous drainage channels to collect water from the area's lakes and marshes. The plan was approved and carried out, and the work was completed in less than two years. Its effects were disastrous. All three of the new cuts were inadequate to contain the rivers that had been diverted into them: areas that had rarely been inundated began to suffer destructive and fatal flooding.

The King soon saw that the drainage scheme would not supply the cash he needed. He rid himself of the Chase within a very few years by pressuring Vermuyden and his Participants to buy or lease most of his twenty thousand acres, but for the commoners, who could not turn their backs on the Chase, the drainage was ruinous. Not only did they lose forty thousand acres of common land, including the most productive farmland, but the botched drainage works, by destroying wetlands and flooding pastures, farms, and villages, brought about 'the utter ruin, both of the land and the inhabitants', according to the anonymous author of an 1829 history of Thorne.

From the outset, local opinion had been strongly against the project. The scheme would take tens of thousands of acres out of the hands of local people and undermine the social and economic stability of the area, and, besides, it was planned and financed, and would be carried out, by foreigners. Feeling against the Dutch workers was so strong that Vermuyden had to establish a separate colony for them, on an island in the Idle River; they would not have been safe in any of the area's villages. In 1626, local people expressed their anger in violent uprisings against the Dutch. The rebellion included most of the local worthies, including Squire Portington, who had accompanied Prince Henry on his fateful reconnoitre of the Chase twenty years earlier. In 1629, Vermuyden laid a complaint against 'the riotous and rebellious carriage of Robert Portington, Esq., and others in beating, wounding, and killing divers of the workmen employed in this undertaking; and for spoiling the walls made for the draining of the lands'. Not relying on fighting alone, the commoners of Hatfield Chase and the Isle of Axholme also petitioned the Crown, claiming that the land had been unfairly divided after the drainage. In 1630, the King's Council for the North, headed by Viscount Wentworth, found that the land had indeed been inequitably distributed, and ordered the Dutch to relinquish some of the land they had claimed. The 'tenants and inhabitants' of Hatfield Chase were awarded Thorne Moors, Hatfield Moors and some smaller areas – a total of almost fifteen thousand acres. The council not only gave the petitioners certain rights over that land but even made them joint owners of it. On 26 July, 1698, Abraham de la Pryme wrote in his diary, 'Our common is freehold unto us, and the lord [of the manor] has nothing to do with it. We have a charter for the same.' The validity of the charter, or deed, was confirmed by the House of Lords in 1758, in response to an attempt by Lord Irwin, then lord of the manor of Hatfield, to assert control over the area.

The revolts over the drainage of Hatfield Chase fit into a tradition of wetlands rebellion. The landscape architect Jeremy Purseglove notes in his book 'Taming the Flood', published in 1988, that 'the English wetlands have a long history as centres of resistance'. Five years after William the Conqueror vanquished the rest of England, he was still struggling to subdue the Cambridgeshire fens. The Peasants' Revolt of 1381 began in the Essex marshlands. John Wesley, who broke away from the Church of England in 1738 to preach Methodism, was born and raised in Epworth, a village about six miles from Thorne. When the English Civil War broke out, in 1642, Thorne and the surrounding villages sided with the Parliamentarians against the King, and hundreds of villagers seized the opportunity to reclaim land that had been taken away from them during the draining. John Lilburne, the flamboyant revolutionary who led the radical democratic party known as the Levellers, came to the Chase and led some of these uprisings.

Despite Vermuyden's problems and failures, his drainage works changed Hatfield Chase for ever. From then on, the push for drainage was unstoppable, though several centuries passed before the change was complete. As the Chase was transformed from wild wetlands into dry fields, the people who lived there were transformed, too, from marshmen into farmers. And, in a process that has been repeated in this century's Third World agricultural-development programmes, as farming became more intensive and productive it also became more expensive – an activity open only to those who could afford to make substantial investments in land. As long as

Hatfield Chase remained pasture and marsh, everyone had been content to treat it as a common resource, but once major drains had been installed it became possible, though expensive, to turn large areas of it from pasture to arable cropland. The land now became worth investing in, worth owning, and those with the capital to pay for improvements managed to acquire it, whether by purchase, fiat, force, or deception. The process was speeded up in the early eighteen-hundreds, when steam pumps made it possible to drain parts of the Chase that had previously proved intractable. Around the same time, a series of parliamentary acts gave certain private individuals the right to enclose large parts of Hatfield Chase's common land. By the mid-nineteenth century, Thorne Moors was the only significant area of common land left on the Chase.

From the time of the Wentworth judgment, in 1630, Thorne Moors was under the administration of elected overseers. The main activities on the moors were still hunting, fishing, and peat gathering. In 1848, however, a well-connected local civil engineer named Makin Durham thought he could make the moors more profitable. He persuaded the overseers, who were legally responsible for the common land, to form the Thorne Moors Improvement Company, for the purpose of turning thousands of acres of peat bog into farmland by draining them and spreading fertile river silt over them – a process known loc- ally as warping. It was an immense task, which would require the construction of a railway across the moors to transport the soil. The warping railway was never built, however, and only a few acres were ever warped.

In 1879, a certain A L Peace, whose overlapping duties as Durham's assistant in the Thorne Moors Improvement Company, chairman of the Thorne overseers, and chairman of the Thorne Parish Council are indicative of the concentration of power that flourished in rural England in those days, transferred ownership of Thorne Moors from the commoners to Thorne Moors Improve- ment Company. Legally or not, Thorne Moors was now in private hands, with no protests from the once-rebellious marshmen of the area. They had become farmers, and were ready to accept what then seemed inevitable – that those wild wetlands would soon be replaced by placid fields of wheat and corn. The men of Thorne were wrong, however. It was peat cutting, not farming, that lay ahead for the moors.

Since medieval times, people had taken peat for fuel from the margins of Thorne Moors, but the impact of these cuttings was small: the bog was undamaged and continued to grow higher. In the early nineteenth century, William Harrison, a miller and botanist, told a friend that when he moved to Thorne 'he could stand on his own threshold and see Crowle Church across the Moors, but such had been the rapid rise of the surface in a comparatively short period, that the sacred edifice had become obscured from view'. In the eighteen-eighties, peat came into commercial demand as a bedding material for animals – a substitute for straw. The Thorne Moors Improvement Company leased Thorne Moors to several peat companies. The companies' first task was to drain their cutting areas, but draining even a small section was a laborious and uncertain process. The area was still boggy, and very difficult to work in and to travel over: ditchdiggers had to wear fen boards to prevent them from sinking into the ground as they worked. Once the top few feet had been drained sufficiently, labourers using sharp-bladed shovels cut blocks of peat from three-foot-wide trenches. The blocks were lifted out and left beside the trenches for a year or more to dry. The dried peat was then hauled off the moors on paths made of clinker – a mixture of charcoal, limestone, and metal ore that is the residue of blast-furnace operations. A Dutch company operating on Thorne Moors also built a series of canals and clinker towpaths, so that horses could pull barges of peat to the moors' edge.

The drainage that precedes peat cutting drives out plants and animals that require a high water table to survive. Species adapted to the harsh conditions of peat bogs are often specialized and rare, and thus are especially vulnerable to extinction. The mire pill beetle spends virtually its entire life under the surface of the wet peat, feeding solely on the leaves of mosses. One of Britain's most severely endangered plants, the rannock rush, which grows only in waterlogged soils, was discovered on Thorne Moors in 1831; less than fifty years later, drainage had banished it from the moors. It survives today at only one site in Britain.

Drainage not only can affect the plants and animals that live on a peat bog but also can change the character of the bog itself. The essence of an acid peat bog – what enables it to maintain its acidic condition – is its wetness. Once the soil dries out, plants die and decay as they would in any other habitat. The nutrients supplied by the decayed plant matter change the bog from a low-nutrient, acid habitat to a nutrient-rich, alkaline one. Nor can the effects of severe drainage be reversed by returning water to the bog. Although peat in its bog is extremely water-retentive, it is extremely difficult to re-wet once it dries out. Even heavy rains will not penetrate dried-out peat. Pumping river water into a drained bog would not help, either, because the river's nutrients would change the bog from an acid environment to an alkaline one, unsuitable for the sphagnum mosses that are the basis of a peat bog.

The peat operations in the nineteenth and early twentieth centuries certainly changed Thorne Moors, but they were not efficient enough to do permanent damage to most of the areas where peat was cut. One reason was that the peat companies did not have the technology to drain or excavate the moors deeply; another was that the large uncut areas alongside every cutting trench were a refuge for the moors' plants and animals. Thus, when the peat cutters finished with a trench and abandoned it, there was enough peat, water and nearby wildlife for the trench to resume its life as part of a healthy, growing peat bog. As it happened, the main impact of this phase of peat cutting was not to destroy the peat bog but to increase the variety of habitats on the moors. Thanks to the limestone-based clinker brought in to provide a solid foundation for tracks and towpaths, new flora and fauna colonized parts of Thorne Moors. Along these tracks now is an alkaline fen, inhabited by marsh orchids and reed warblers, side by side with the carnivorous bladderworts and heath butter-flies of the acid bog. After this wave of peat cutting, Thorne Moors was no longer a pristine raised bog, but it did re-main a rich, robust habitat.

In the early part of this century, the automobile gradually supplanted the horse, and the market for peat as a bedding material for animals declined. Peat extraction on Thorne Moors continued through the nineteen-thirties, forties, and fifties, but in a slow, old-fashioned way: the peat was cut by hand and hauled off the moors in horse-drawn wagons. That was the state of affairs when an irascible, uncompromising man named William Bunting arrived in Thorne. Bunting was born in 1916 in Barnsley, a working-class coal-mining town twenty miles west of Thorne, where his parents were greengrocers. He left school at sixteen and became an engineer's fitter, making and mending machines and tools in a succession of jobs.

31

During the Spanish Civil War, Bunting was a courier for the *Reynolds News*, a left-wing Sunday paper, and he smuggled money and messages to the Anarchists. His experiences during that period led to his carrying out several undercover jobs for the British government on the Continent in the Second World War, notably in Yugoslavia. At the end of the war, Bunting and his wife and family settled in Thorne.

Fascinated by the moors, Bunting became a self-taught naturalist – and a respected one. He is a member of the Royal Entomological Society, a specialist in insect physiology, and the author of papers on such topics as viper embryos, freshwater shrimp, and bloodworms. Among his discoveries is *Lyngbya thornensis*, a species of alga that lives on the antennae of microscopic water fleas. His discoveries on the moors go beyond biology, however. According to Paul Buckland, a paleoecologist at the University of Sheffield, who has done most of the work on the archaeology of moors around Thorne, it was Bunting who, in 1971, first drew attention to the Bronze Age wooden pathway under Thorne Moors. Bunting was also the first person to put forward, in a paper written in 1969, the view, now accepted, that the northern arm of the River Don is actually an artificial channel, probably constructed by the Romans.

Bunting spent a lot of time walking Thorne Moors and studying its wildlife. He soon became convinced that the area was of great scientific and ecological value, but his claims on its behalf were widely dismissed. The conventional wisdom was that farming and peat digging had already ruined Thorne Moors – had destroyed its once fascinating flora and fauna. In those days, Thorne Moors was generally regarded as an underutilized piece of wasteland. In 1962, the South Yorkshire County Council considered a plan to use it as a dumping ground for ash from coal-fired power plants. Five years later, the council proposed filling in the moors with mining slag and other industrial waste and then putting an airport on top. In 1969, the plan to dump ash from power plants was reintroduced. In 1971, planners revived the airport idea. In 1976, the ash plan reared its head a third time, along with a third proposal for an airport. In 1978, a plan to reopen a disused coal mine at the edge of the moor carried with it a threat to dump colliery waste on the moors. Bunting fought fiercely against every one of these propos-als, and all of them were eventually defeated.

In his championing of Thorne Moors, Bunting at first had little help from established conservation groups: they dismissed him as an abrasive amateur. In 1969, the county's leading wildlife group, the Yorkshire Naturalists' Trust, voted not to object to the plan to dump fuel ash on the moors. Bunting, outraged, mounted a campaign to get the trust to change its mind. He wrote scathing letters, compiled reports, and badgered the organization's leading lights to come and see for themselves. In his words, 'I took them on to the moor and rubbed their noses in it.' On one

Bunting-led outing, a group from the trust found, among other things, twelve species of mushrooms not previously thought to grow on Thorne Moors. After four months, the trust reversed itself and voted to defend the moors. Wilfred Taylor, the president of the trust, wrote to Bunting, saying, 'We well know that the credit for most of the resistance to this threat is entirely due to your efforts and to the immense amount of work and expense you have gone to in past years.'

Bunting also had to fight the Nature Conservancy Council, the government body responsible for conservation, which had denied for many years that there was anything of interest on Thorne Moors, and made no objection to the plans for using it as a dumping ground. The council is understaffed and underfinanced and has little political clout, but Bunting disregards these facts and has nothing but contempt for its compromising ways. 'The biggest opponents to preserving the place, the biggest opponents all the way through, were the Nature Conservancy,' he told me not long ago. 'When people wanted to dump ash on Thorne Moors, they never made a bloody squeak.' For years, he hounded the council, demanding, without success, that it give official protection to Thorne Moors. In 1970, the council finally did list Thorne Moors as one of Britain's most important habitats, awarding it the unappealing official title of Site of Special Scientific Interest. Unfortunately, that designation,though it is almost the highest that a valuable habitat can receive, is largely

34

symbolic. In the case of Thorne Moors, it is no hindrance to Fisons' intensive peat extraction.

In 1963, Fisons acquired the British Moss Litter Company, which was the eventual successor to the Thorne Moors Improvement Company, and began promoting peat as a replacement for garden compost. The campaign was a success. It rejuvenated the peat industry and led to its mechanization. The first machines still cut peat in blocks, as the hand cutters had done, but they cut faster and required more efficient and intensive, and thus more destructive, drainage. In late 1971, Fisons excavated several deep drains that threatened to destroy completely the Dutch Canal part of Thorne Moors, which is the richest part of the area. Bunting, who had long urged that the Dutch Canal area be made a National Nature Reserve, and others were alarmed. One ecologist reported that 'it is unlikely that these communities' – of plants and animals – 'will survive a summer with such a low water table'. With the heart of the moors at risk, Bunting and a group of naturalists, local residents, and students from a number of northern universities, including Sheffield, York, Nottingham, and Manchester, decided to take matters into their own hands. Calling themselves Bunting's Beavers, the group went on to the moors practically every weekend throughout the spring and summer of 1972 to dam the drains, using stones, peat, clay, logs, and even railway sleepers. Fisons' workers made an effort to remove the dams, but were unable to keep up with the Beavers, and by the early autumn of 1972 dozens of dams had been built, some of them more than forty feet thick.

In late October of 1972, shortly after a BBC television crew filmed the Beavers at work, Fisons dynamited 18 of the dams. The Beavers repaired them, and Fisons, which had been showered with unfavourable publicity, let the new dams stand. The company then entered into negotiations (from which Bunting was specifically excluded) with the Conservancy Council and a group of ecologists from northern universities. The result, in 1974, was an agreement by the company to protect the Dutch Canal area from drainage and cutting. The agreement required Fisons to reinforce several of the dams that the Beavers had installed. Eleven years later, the Nature Conservancy Council bought a hundred and eighty acres of the Dutch Canal system from Fisons for a price rumoured to be a quarter of a million pounds and declared it a National Nature Reserve. The area is now safe from cutting, but it is far too small to support on its own the full range of plants and animals that live on the moors, and it will survive only as long as the water table of the surrounding land is kept high.

One reason that Thorne Moors had so few defenders in the nineteen-fifties and sixties was that after the war few people had first-hand knowledge of the place. The paths that had crossed the moors in earlier days had been obstructed or destroyed by landowners or tenants. Under

English law, the public has the right to walk along hundreds of thousands of ancient lanes and footpaths, even if they cross private property. This extensive system of public access is one of the glories of the British country-side, but it has been seriously eroded by property owners' illegally eliminating or blocking footpaths that cross their land. The Second World War intensified this process, as Britain's Ministry of Agriculture, worried about the nation's dependence on imported grain, pushed hard for a more intensive agriculture. Across the country, millions of acres of pastureland were converted to arable cropland, and in the process thousands of footpaths were ploughed up.

In 1949, Parliament attempted to rectify this state of affairs by adopting the National Park and Access to the Countryside Act. The act was intended to halt the destruction of footpaths by creating a definitive register of all public rights-of-way, so that they could be protected for evermore. Unfortunately, the effect of the law was to accelerate the destruction of rights-of-way, for many landowners rushed to eliminate public footpaths from their land before they could be registered. 'During this period, footpaths and in many cases very wide country lanes which had been known and used for ever suddenly ceased to exist,' Bunting later wrote. 'Barbed wire was strung across highways – footpaths ploughed up . . . and anyone trying to use these public ways would find themselves in confrontation with farmers and others who aggressively attacked all or any to prevent them going about their lawful business. Complaints to the police fell upon deaf ears.'

Bunting, of course, continued to walk the old footpaths. Whenever he encountered one that was blocked, he opened it, using wire cutters that he always wore at his waist. Before moving on, he posted his business card at the site. 'It wasn't vandalism,' he told me. 'I was exercising my rights, and I had no wish to hide my identity. Let the buggers sue me if they dare.' Bunting talks tough, and he occasionally acts tough, too. When he goes out on the moors, he carries a gun, a walking stick that conceals a razor-sharp sabre, a machete, and his wire cutters. If he is threatened by a fist or a bullet – and, according to several witnesses, he has encountered more than a few of both – he returns like for like. 'Any person who takes a liberty with me never does it a second time,' he told me. When I asked if he had ever had occasion to fire a gun while walking the moors, he roared, 'What do you think I use them for, picking my bloody nose? If any bugger shoots at me or threatens my life, I've got the absolute right to defend myself.'

Bunting also hectored the authorities about enforcing the footpath laws. In an unpublished statement called 'How It All Started' Bunting has written, 'Every day . . . and I mean EVERY DAY I wrote in longhand to the County Council reporting on the obstructions etc. I met. I was always assured the matters would be put right. . . . In desperation I started using a typewriter and keeping copies.' The last straw for Bunting came in 1952, when the West Riding County Council published its footpath map, and the map showed no public rights-of-way on Thorne Moors. Even today, almost forty years later, Bunting gets nearly apoplectic when he talks of the omission: 'I knew there were bloody footpaths – I'd used 'em!' Bunting set out to get protection for those footpaths. He was embarking on a thirty-year battle, trading long days on the moors for days and nights spent in libraries, archives, record offices, and courtrooms. He began by acquainting himself with the confused and arcane laws and administrative regulations on public rights-of-way. Gradually, he extended his knowledge to details of other public rights.

Bunting's first foray into the legal world was on his own behalf. It began in 1954, when his landlord, which happened to be the Thorne Rural District Council, evicted him from his house for breeding cockroaches there. At the time, Bunting, who had been unfit for work since 1948, because he had tuberculosis, was earning about three hundred pounds a year by supplying schools and universities with biological-research materials, including specimens of the American cockroach (*Periplaneta americana*), a large and thus easy-to-study species much valued in insect-physiology courses. He kept several thousand roaches in twelve glass-topped tanks in the family's living room. A health inspector found that the setup violated no sanitary standards, but the council decided that the roaches had to go – and Bunting and his family with them.

Newspapers leapt on the story and ran it day after day. The Yorkshire *Evening Post* described Bunting as 'Cockroach Man'; in the Doncaster *Gazette* he was 'Beetle Man'; *The Times*, then still the respected 'newspaper of record', took a more sober line, referring to 'Entomologist in Cockroach Case.' The Royal Entomological Society, the National Council for Civil Liberties, and the Society for Freedom in Science all lodged appeals on Bunting's behalf, to no avail. On 9 July, 1954, the bailiffs ousted Bunting, his wife, and their five children. 'COCKROACH BREEDER EVICTED,' *The Times* announced the following morning. For some time, the family was split up, billeted with various friends and relatives. When they finally found a new home, Bunting – in a move that amused half the town and irritated almost all the council – named it Periplaneta.

Bunting applied for damages, and pursued the case to the High Court of Justice. The judge, Hugh Hallett, ruled against him. During the hearing, Hallett barely troubled to disguise his contempt for Bunting's defiant manner and blunt language. When Bunting asked to be affirmed rather than sworn in before testifying, explaining to the judge, 'I am an atheist,' Hallett added, 'And no morals, either.' He also called Bunting 'a slippery character' and 'a troublemaking agitator.' People who have run-ins with Bunting are not likely to escape unscathed, and Hallett was no exception. In 1957, Bunting took his complaints about the judge's behaviour to the Court of Appeal. The hearing ran for days and ended with an order for a new trial and a humiliating rebuke for Hallett – one which contributed to his resignation later that year. Bunting soon became a one-man legal-advice bureau for people unable to pay a lawyer. 'If you'd got a grievance with the local authority, the first person you used to go to was William Bunting,' Roland Smalley, a retired mechanic who has known Bunting all his life, told me. 'He was a sort of self-taught professor of all the local laws and bylaws. He caused a lot of trouble and a lot of expense to the council.'

Peter O'Brien, the deputy director of planning for the Doncaster Metropolitan Borough Council, which in 1974 became the successor to the Thorne Rural District Council, recalls, 'He was very difficult, but his knowledge was incredible, and his persistence was also incredible.' Indeed, Bunting was so troublesome to bureaucrats endeavouring to close footpaths, ignore sewage problems, build unneeded airports, route motorways through nature reserves, and dump toxic waste on important wildlife habitats that for many years local council officials were forbidden to speak to him or to take his phone calls. Communications with him were funnelled through a handful of top executives. Nonetheless, as one Borough Council official ruefully told me, 'he's taken the local authority to the cleaners so many times.' And not only the local council. Bunting has also taken on and beaten such powerful national forces as British Rail, the Forestry Commission, and the National Coal Board.

To further his campaigns, Bunting taught himself law.

He has argued and won several cases before the High Court of Justice – a feat that eludes the majority of professional lawyers. He also taught himself Latin, medieval English, and Norman French – languages that come in handy when basing legal arguments, as Bunting has often done, on documents from the sixteenth century or earlier. Bunting broke legal ground when, arguing from the Magna Carta, he made the High Court Chancery Division travel to Yorkshire to hear a lawsuit he was involved in – the first time in the court's eight-hundred-year history that it had left London. Like many of his cases, that one concerned Thorne Moors.

For the past thirty years, Bunting has been legally bankrupt. He chose this status deliberately, so that he would be free to fight his legal battles without worrying about being sued. The house he and his wife live in is owned by two of his children. He has given away the legal costs and settlements he has been awarded, which have sometimes been substantial. 'I remember him sending an envelope here for the cancer-research fund containing quite a lot of cash that he'd just got,' I was told by Margaret Prosser, longtime secretary to the late Harry Fairhurst, who was the chief librarian at York University and one of Bunting's academic supporters. 'It wasn't a little sum. I said, "Look at that," and Harry said, "Oh, yes, he gives it." ' That happened back in the sixties, and during the same period Mark Williamson, a professor in York University's Department of Biology, recalls, Bunting 'was so broke that he used to type with a red ribbon – he would get secondhand typewriter ribbons where the black was gone but the red was still OK'.

Much harder for Bunting to bear than his self-imposed poverty has been his ill health. Shortly after the war, he was found to be suffering from spondylitis, a crippling inflammation of the vertebrae. For long periods, drugs and an iron will enabled him to lead a normal, active life, despite this and a variety of other debilitating ailments. John Barwick, the director of the Doncaster Museum, remembers the first time he spoke to Bunting. 'It was at the 1956 meeting of the British Association for the Advancement of Science,' he said. 'Bunting's daughter was only nineteen at the time, but she was delivering a paper about the sex life of the American cockroach. Television was new then, and the room was packed with reporters and cameramen who were fascinated by this innocent young girl addressing a roomful of scientists on this strange topic. And, of course, the eviction case was still going through the courts, so it was brilliant publicity for Bunting. I was standing outside the conference room when a horribly twisted figure, really distorted, came hobbling up. It was Bunting. He looked so pitiful I asked if he'd like a wheelchair. He just looked at me and growled, "I'd let air into my veins first." '

Though Bunting can be, in the words of Peter Skidmore, the Doncaster Museum's Keeper of Natural Sciences, 'the epitome of the English gentleman', he is often insufferably rude, even to his friends. 'I'm a bad-tempered old sod,' he says, and so he frequently is. There are two parts to Bunting's rudeness, and they are equally unpalatable: his own natural arrogance and a calculated offensiveness he uses to test the mettle of enemies and allies alike. He subjects correspondents, interviewers, and would-be supporters to a formidable series of hurdles from a seemingly inexhaustible supply. His speech is peppered with curses and obscenities, employed as much for their shock value as for their expressiveness. Anyone who buckles under this treatment is summarily dismissed: Bunting has no time for wimps. In a letter to a colleague in 1979, he described his treatment of Jane Smart, who is now the director of the plant conservation group Plantlife; at the time she approached Bunting, she was a student at the University of Sheffield, working toward a doctorate in the ecology of peat bogs. 'If she can be put off by Bunting at his rudest and crudest . . . well, I did my best to put her off,' Bunting wrote. 'If she comes back she will be helped [and] she will certainly have earned my assistance.' Smart did return, and Bunting agreed to take her out on the moors, on condition she prove that she could fire a pistol.

Bunting makes no attempt to conceal his contempt for those who fail to live up to his standards: they are 'corrupt', 'pea-brained', 'charlatans', or 'prats'. John Barwick says, 'Bunting doesn't have much sense of the practical limitations many people are under from their job or their circumstances. If they don't do what he thinks is right, they're corrupt, as far as he's concerned. That puts a lot of people's backs up.' Peter Skidmore agrees. 'You can't have an attitude like Bunting's without polarizing people,' he says. 'I mean, either you're strongly in favour of him or you're dead against him.' Nonetheless, Bunting has won many unlikely allies over the years. One is Paula Haigh, a smallholder, retired headmistress, and local Conservative Party councillor. 'With Bunting, everything is subservient to the cause,' she has said. 'That's why we admire him, and put up with his language. Because we admire what he stands for, if not the way he stands for it.'

Bunting's grumpiness is to some extent a pose – a way of stiffening the backs of conservationists, most of whom he believes to be far too pliable, too complacent, too willing to bargain away what is left of mankind's heritage. To a young man who asked for his help in developing a compromise over the plan to dump toxic waste on a nearby marsh, Bunting replied, 'I suggest that the essence of conservation lies with one simple word, NO. . . . Don't become like those prostitutes in the Nature Conservancy. Say NO . . . mean NO . . . fight to retain the places we have.'

Over the years, Bunting discovered a taste and an aptitude for research and archival work. The High Court judge David Herbert Mervyn Davies has called him 'a learned man in the matter of tracing and expounding local historical documents'. Bunting's approach has been more robust than that of most archivists, who tend to be a mild-mannered lot. He has refused to take no for an answer, particular when, as has often happened, he believes that public documents are being wrongly withheld. 'I had to fight the buggers physically, some of them,' he once told me. 'I grabbed them by the throat and said, "If you don't find the damn things, I'll find them over your body." But I made them find the bloody things.'

Bunting is genuinely excited by original source material. Not long ago, describing a set of detailed maps he had discovered that show land ownership throughout the country, his voice fell to an awestruck hush, and he said, 'Twenty-five inches to the mile – for every part of England!' County councils across the nation have adopted a method of determining the existence of rights-of-way which is based on what one archivist calls Bunting's 'pioneering research' on official records. Bunting also unearthed a long-lost account of the Dutch drainage of Hatfield Chase, and was instrumental in its being republished and deposited in various libraries throughout Britain. Though most of his papers have already gone to York University and other libraries ('BUGMAN PAPERS GO TO 'VARSITY,' ' read the headline in the Doncaster *Star*), his study is still awash in documents – parish records, seventeenth-century court orders in spidery script, and ancient maps.

Bunting's archival work led him to try to restore Thorne Moors to common-land status. His effort began in

1952, when he went to the Thorne library to study the town's old records. In 'How It All Started' he recorded what happened next. The caretaker 'eventually produced them, two beautiful books dealing with the period from 1817 to 1895,' he wrote. 'I found much of what I was looking for.' The following day, Bunting returned to the library to continue studying the books and was told by the librarian, who was also Thorne's town clerk, that the books could be seen only by appointment. He made an appointment to return the next day. When he was handed the books, he found that 'the oldest of the two had been mutilated, back broken, pages missing', his account continues. 'The later book did not appear to be damaged until one tried to read, then it was noticed that complete pages had been removed . . . further on some pages had been crudely cut out.'

Bunting became convinced that the books were damaged in an attempt to hide the illegal transfer of the moors from the overseers to private owners in 1879. Whatever their ancestors' feelings about the transfer – and Bunting says that local comment was stifled because Thorne's leaders were all in on the deal – most people in Thorne long ago accepted the fact that Thorne Moors is now in private hands. Bunting does not. The deed conveying Thorne Moors to the Thorne Moors Improvement Company 'is blatantly fraudulent', he says. 'They'd never heard of it at the Public Record Office; they hadn't heard of it in the County Clerk of the Peace's office, which has to have copies of every land transaction.' Thorne's past is real to Bunting, and a century-old wrong is as obnoxious to him as if it had happened yesterday. He often talks about historical events as if he had been part of the action. Telling me about Lord Irwin's attempt to gain control of Thorne Moors, in the mid-eighteenth century, he spoke as one of the commoners: 'There was a court case, and when we were asked for our charter we couldn't produce it, because the agent for the lord of the manor was suppressing it.'

Throughout British history, there have been many cases of powerful landowners' simply appropriating common land, and the legal status of many areas that were once common land is confused. In 1965, Parliament adopted the Commons Registration Act, under which only those areas that were registered by the government before a certain date would be legally recognized as common land – land over which the public has certain specified rights. The Thorne Parish Council decided to apply to register the moors and asked for Bunting's help in doing so. Despite objections from Fisons and from the more powerful Thorne Rural District Council, Bunting submitted the parish council's application for registration in 1968, along with identical applications that he had prepared on behalf of himself, his wife and his son, Neil. The rural district council took the Buntings to court in an effort to force them to drop their applications. The matter went to the High Court, which supported Bunting, and the registrations remained in force. The parish council, however, was finally pressured into withdrawing its registration; it did so in 1973, on the last day that changes were allowed. From then on, Bunting was fighting for the commons on his own. He added an eighteenth-century verse to his visiting card:

The law locks up the man or woman
Who steals the goose from off the common.
But lets the greater villain loose
Who steals the common off the goose.

In 1976, the Commons Commissioner, Alfred Baden-Fuller, ruled against Bunting's application to register Thorne Moors as common land. Baden-Fuller is someone for whom Bunting has nothing but scorn. 'As a person who could not read seventeenth-century English, he was totally unfit,' Bunting later remarked. Bunting appealed on the finding to the High Court, but his hearing was delayed until 1983. By that time he was suffering from pernicious anaemia, and his other illnesses had seriously worsened.

Wearing a surgical collar that stretched from his breast-bone to his chin, and unable, because of spondylitis, to sit for long periods, he stood before the judge for as long as eight hours each day during a ten-day hearing. On several occasions, he collapsed in court.

Bunting seems to have enjoyed cordial relations with Justice Mervyn Davies, who was impressed by his knowledge of history and law. Their polite exchanges entertained the courtroom and the reporters covering the case. As Bunting introduced documents from the sixteenth century and earlier, the judge remarked, 'Quite interesting, eh, Mr. Bunting, to see these old historical figures emerging?'

'Indeed,' Bunting replied. 'Sir Francis Bacon was involved and he was sacked for corruption, and I can bring an ancestor of mine in who was sent to Australia.'

On another occasion, Bunting began, 'Turning to the decree of 1609 . . .'

'Shouldn't it be 1610?' the judge asked. 'It is the seventh year of the reign of James I, who came to the throne in 1603.'

'Ah, but the seventh regnal year of James I started on 24 March, 1609,' Bunting replied. 'The decree is quite clearly 1609.'

When Bunting referred to Fisons' high-powered barrister, Raymond Kidwell, as 'my learned adversary', Mervyn Davies asked, 'Don't you mean "my learned friend"?'

'No, my lord,' Bunting said firmly. 'I mean adversary. I am not of your profession.'

Bunting won the case. The court found that he had established that the commoners of Thorne had the right to turbary - the medieval term for peat cutting – over Thorne Moors, and ordered Fisons to pay Bunting's legal costs. Since Bunting was the only commoner to have applied to have his rights recognized, however, he was the only person to whom they were granted. The judge's decision was only a partial victory, for several reasons. One was

the judge's refusal to consider whether or not Fisons' title
to the land was based on fraud, as Bunting claimed.
Another was the judge's finding that in the seventeenth
century the residents of Thorne had traded away many
rights over the land, including the right to fish, hunt, and
graze cattle on the moors. If those rights, and especially
the right to graze, had been recognized, they would have
interfered with Fisons' peat-cutting operations. As it is, the
peat cutting goes on, and Fisons is confident that Bunting's
right of turbary, which attaches to him and to all future
owners of his house in Thorne, will not hinder its peat extraction or influence its future plans for the moors.

Bunting is old now, and very ill. He is afflicted not only
with spondylitis and pernicious anaemia but also with
dropsy and near-total blindness. In 1989, he had four
strokes. 'My wife keeps picking me up off the floor,' he
told me. He believes that an appeal to have more of the
ancient rights recognized could succeed but says he won't
be the man to pursue it. He would like 'someone with
guts' to take over the house and continue the legal battle,
he says. It is not only courage that is required, however,
but also commitment and a grasp of the complex legal and
historical issues involved – a commitment and a grasp
that no one but Bunting seems to have.

By the time Bunting's case was settled, in the mid-
nineteen-eighties, the effects of twenty years of peat

extraction from Thorne Moors were disturbingly clear. A survey published in 1986 by the Doncaster and District Ornithological Society concluded that 'the past fifteen years have seen a change from a scientifically rich and inspiring moorland, with additional appeal beyond the confines of science, to a fragmented habitat with vulnerable wildlife, which could now so easily turn into a wasteland'. Among the species that disappeared from the area during that period were the fen violet and the carnivorous long-leaved sundew.

But the most dramatic damage to the moors was still to come. In 1987, Fisons introduced a new technology – surface milling. Instead of taking blocks of peat from narrow trenches, surface-milling machines skim a thin layer of peat from a very large area, hundreds of acres in extent, and skim additional layers every few weeks. Before a peat bog can be milled, it must be deep-drained and the top layer of living vegetation must be scraped off to expose the peat. Thus, though the area to be milled may have a twenty-year supply of peat, the living bog is destroyed in the first year. Surface milling has been the norm in Canada, Russia, Finland, and Ireland since the nineteen-sixties or earlier. 'Fisons were about the last to adopt surface milling,' I was told by Donal Egan, who managed the company's Thorne Moors operation until his resignation, in December 1990. 'If we had been earlier, we might not have a problem about Thorne Moors, because it wouldn't be worth fighting for.' Already, surface milling has turned great expanses of

Thorne Moors into utterly barren ground – marked only by tractor lines stretching away to the horizon. Fisons says the peat of Thorne Moors can be milled for at least forty years longer. But milling will destroy the area's wildlife long before all the peat is removed. 'The way they're working the moor now, you can see them wiping out the interest – well, in not many more years,' one worried Doncaster council official told me.

To accommodate its new machines, Fisons is draining the moors faster than ever. In 1989 alone, the company installed twenty-two miles of deep drains on Thorne Moors, more than doubling the existing deep-drainage system. Because these drains are cut into the underlying clay and silts, they are incredibly dangerous. They not only dry out the bog but also contaminate its acidic water table with nutrients that many peat-adapted species cannot tolerate. 'Fisons have done more damage in the last two years than since they owned the moors. They've put in more drains than ever in the history of the moors,' the Sheffield University paleoecologist Paul Buckland, who has studied the moors for almost twenty years, told me. In the spring of 1990, Fisons also ended Thorne Moors' run as the largest roadless area in lowland Britain by putting a three-mile-long road made of crushed limestone through the middle of the moors. The alkaline dust from the road, which is from thirty to fifty feet wide, is likely to damage the bog's alkali-intolerant species. According to Brian Eversham, the son of a Thorne peat worker and now a peatland ecologist who works for the locally financed Institute of Terrestrial Ecology, 'Thorne Moors is being destroyed so fast that in only one or two years we'll be in the position not of preserving an intact habitat but of trying to rebuild a wildlife habitat on a derelict industrial site.'

Even though the moorland is one of Britain's élite Sites of Special Scientific Interest, Fisons is entirely within its legal rights in destroying it, because in 1951 the two local councils that have jurisdiction over Thorne Moors granted the company permission for peat cutting over almost the whole area. 'It's probably the largest single planning permission in the country, and there are no restrictions on it,' a Doncaster council spokesman told me. 'All they've got to do is keep within the boundary.' Unfortunately, Fisons has found that impossible. Outside the peat-extraction boundary was a small area of undisturbed bog – Snaith and Cowick Moors. That area is part of the Site of Special Scientific Interest, and was the home of several species not known on the rest of Thorne Moors, including the grizzled skipper butterfly and stag's-horn club moss. Fisons illegally drained Snaith and Cowick and cut peat from it for more than a decade. In 1988 the local authorities discovered the work and asked the company to stop. The peat cutting destroyed much of the area's conservation interest: eliminating stag's-horn club moss, for example. The Nature Conservancy Council could have prosecuted Fisons for taking peat illegally from a Site of

Special Scientific Interest, but one of the many loopholes in British wildlife-protection legislation makes companies and individuals immune to such prosecution as soon as they apply, as Fisons has, for retroactive planning permission to take peat from the site. Fisons has offered to compensate the Nature Conservancy Council by giving it a hundred and thirteen acres of already drained and cut-over land adjacent to the National Nature Reserve, and the conservancy is ready to accept the offer, but conservationists consider it inadequate.

Such incidents and the new and shocking sight of hundreds of acres of stripped-bare land have convinced many people that the government should step in and stop peat extraction on the moorland. 'If the government asked the advice of Brian Wheeler and Jane Smart and me and the other peat experts, we'd say leave as much peat as possible, compensate Fisons, and have Fisons follow our instructions to leave the bog so that it can recover,' I was told by David Bellamy, a peatland ecologist and well-known TV conservationist. Friends of the Earth and Plantlife are calling for a ban on peat cutting on all Sites of Special Scientific Interest, and for a review of all planning permits for peat extraction. Drastic as that may sound, West Germany did something similar in 1972. It withdrew all existing mineral licences, including those for peat extraction, without compensation. Companies were required to apply for new licences, and those were issued with strict conditions governing methods of extractions and standards for restoration.

Under British law, however, a licence to extract peat cannot be revoked unless the owner is compensated for all profits forgone. In the case of Thorne Moors, Donal Egan says, that would amount to more than a hundred million pounds. Faced with such huge sums, the Doncaster Metropolitan Borough Council, which is the local planning authority, has little or no leverage over Fisons' peat operations. Though the council has been pressing the company to manage Thorne Moors so that the bog will not be permanently damaged, progress in such discussions depends largely on Fisons' good will. The Nature Conservancy Council – being without strong backing from central government – is equally at Fisons' mercy. Confidential official minutes of a Nature Conservancy Council meeting about Thorne Moors in 1977 quote the council's regional officer as saying, 'The NCC has to go along with Fisons, to humour them, and to hope for better circumstances in the future.'

I asked an official in the Department of the Environment – which in addition to overseeing conservation in England regulates peat extraction – whether the Secretary of State for the Environment would get involved in the battle over the destruction of one of the country's most important nature-conservation sites. She told me no – in these words:

'The debate [about peat extraction] is not turning upon the solution to an individual site. Rather our general remit is to set down general guidance assessing the extent of peatlands in England and Wales, their relative importance for nature conservation, their importance for peat extraction and the extent to which those interests conflict, and making an updated assessment of alternatives to peat. Whether we should have a new minerals policy guidance paper for peatlands is part of the consideration. This would include principles from which acceptable solutions could be found for individual sites, which is, of course, a matter for individual minerals planning authorities.'

In the spring of 1990, British conservation groups launched a campaign to dissuade the public from buying peat. The campaign has had considerable success, as measured by the degree of publicity it has received. Britain is a nation of gardeners, and 'gardeners go berserk when they discover what they have been helping to destroy,' Jane Smart says. Several local authorities have stopped using peat, declaring themselves 'peat-free zones', and even the Department of the Environment, despite its reluctance to get involved in controversial issues, advises gardeners to 'avoid using peat to improve the soil' saying, 'It is expensive and its extraction can damage the environment.' And the Forestry Commission published a report last March warning that peat is overused in tree planting. Many trees are killed or damaged during dry spells when their peat-based planting compost dries out, the commission reported. Among the converts to the cause is Prince Charles. 'If we would like other countries to stop regarding their rain forests as "useless jungle", ' he said recently, 'we would do well to set an example by not treating our peatland habitat as "useless bog" to be drained, dug up, and scattered about in our gardens.'

Even Bunting's old nemesis, the local council in Thorne, has joined the campaign to save the moors. 'Our next big project is to try and stop Fisons, by public opinion and by getting legal advice,' says Ted Tattersall, a Thorne councillor and longtime Bunting foe. It was local interest in the moors that pushed the council into action, and the local interest was sparked largely by two events. In 1989, many people in the village saw a television programme about Thorne Moors which featured well-known conservationists and gardeners. For the first time, they realized that their local moorland, which they had long taken for granted, was regarded by famous outsiders as being of national importance. At the same time, local conservationists began a programme of guided visits to the National Nature Reserve, enabling people living in and near Thorne to see for themselves both the beauty of the moors and the encroaching devastation. On one of the tours, a grey-haired man who runs a printing shop in Thorne founded by his grandfather told me he had never been on the moors before. 'We weren't allowed,' he said. 'It's always been off-limits.' The others in the group, ranging in age from thirty to seventy, nodded in agreement. Many in the group knew Bunting, or knew of him and his enthusiasm for Thorne Moors. 'If it was now, we'd all be behind him, but then we just laughed at him,' one woman said. 'We didn't understand.'

Ninety per cent of the peat from Thorne Moors is augmented with fertilizers and used as potting compost or in 'grow-bags', which are plastic bags of soil (largely peat) that people put outdoors, cut open, and plant seeds in. The rest is sold straight, for use as a mulch or a soil conditioner. There are many alternatives to straight peat – straw, bark, and rice husks, to name a few – but finding a replacement for peat in potting compost has been more difficult. The obvious alternative is homemade compost, which is what all gardeners used until the horticultural peat industry was born, twenty-five years ago. The convenience of pre-bagged peat has won it a loyal following, especially among city dwellers, including Margaret Thatcher, who proclaimed her loyalty at 1990's Royal Chelsea Flower Show, saying, 'What some of the conservationists would say to us for using peat today I don't know, but I don't know what a gardener can do without peat. I intend to go on using it.' In Switzerland, however, where a national law came into effect in 1991 banning all commercial peat cutting, city composting is common. Donal Egan says that for years Fisons has been searching for an alternative potting material, without luck. But a recently published study that scientists at the University of Manchester undertook for Friends of the Earth concludes that there are several promising alternatives to peat, ranging from leaf mould to composted sewage sludge. One company, Hensby Biotech, in Cambridge, has recently put a peat-free potting compost on the market, and other companies have announced plans to follow suit.

Fisons dominates the peat market in Britain – and ninety per cent of its peat holdings are in Sites of Special Scientific Interest – but the bulk of the company's profits comes from its scientific-equipment division and from its pharmaceutical division, whose products include Sanatogen vitamins and dietary supplements and Desenex foot powder. In 1989, the horticultural division produced less than five per cent of the company's pretax profits, of a hundred and sixty-nine million pounds. Fisons sells peat-based potting mixtures under the Levington brand in Britain and under the Sunshine brand in the United States. The United States has few deep peat bogs, and most of the peat sold there comes from Canada's dwindling bogs.

According to Fisons, the campaign has not affected its peat sales. 'If anything, it has highlighted to many people the benefits of peat,' Egan told me as we sat in his office, near Thorne Moors. 'There has been panic buying in some areas.' The people want peat, Egan says, and there is no reason for them not to have it. 'Apart from some species and wildlife, the use of peat enhances people's lives, it doesn't take away from them,' he said. 'And that is why [the outcry over peat] won't last – because at the end of the day people will ask, "How does it hurt me?" '

Nonetheless, public pressure has had an effect on the company. 'We started talking to Fisons around 1978,' a planning officer for the Doncaster Metropolitan Borough

Council told me. 'But we didn't get anywhere until quite recently. Until then, there was no pressure on them.' Brian Wheeler, a peat specialist from Sheffield University, who has a three-year contract with Fisons to study the regeneration of Thorne Moors, says, 'We've seen a sea change in the attitude at Fisons, from one that was grudging at best about any proposals we made to a completely different attitude, which actually welcomes cooperative action. I think it's a genuine change. I hope it is.'

In response to environmentalists' criticism, the British Peat Producers' Association, of which Fisons is a member, announced on 22 February, 1990, that it was adopting a non-binding code of conduct that would 'encourage peat producers to do all in their power to reduce the impact of their operations on the environment.' The code does not advocate leaving intact peat bogs alone, but it does suggest that peat companies 'identify areas of greater environmental interest and where possible leave them undisturbed' and 'avoid land preparation' – that is, draining and clearing land – 'too far ahead of need.'

A month before the code was unveiled, a consortium of conservation groups concerned about Thorne Moors asked Fisons for permission to survey one of the least disturbed sections of the moorland – a hundred-and-forty-three-acre area known as Pony Bridge Marsh, which was due to be worked in the spring of 1991. Pony Bridge Marsh is the only site on the moors where the rare raft spider has been found. The groups hoped that if Pony Bridge Marsh proved to be as rich as they suspected Fisons would agree to protect it as a biological refuge, in line with the Peat Producers' code of conduct. Fisons agreed to the survey and indicated that it wanted to help pay for it. Then, just six days before the code was announced, Fisons told the groups that it intended to cut Pony Bridge Marsh in the next few months – a year earlier than had been planned. That eliminated the possibility that a full survey could be conducted and that the area might be set aside as a refuge. Two days later, conservationists discovered that Fisons had already drained the marsh. According to Egan, the company had merely 'hacked out' existing drains to make the site safe for survey work, but he acknowledged that 'it did dry the area out somewhat'. Aerial photographs indicate, however, that existing drains had been substantially deepened, and that five miles of new drains had been constructed on the site. After conservationists complained to the Peat Producers' Association, Fisons blocked the drains and agreed to delay its cutting of the marsh until the biological survey could be completed.

Several conservation groups – notably Friends of the Earth and Plantlife – are open in their scepticism about Fisons' good intentions. They charge that the studies the company has commissioned and its negotiations with conservationists are intended merely to buy time so that Fisons can strip what remains of the moors without interference. David Bellamy says, 'Fisons could have done so much over the last twenty-five years. They could have been working away, making little hydrologically healthy pockets and so forth. And the fact that they haven't makes me wonder about what they really plan to do with the land after they've worked it.' Members of the conservation consortium, which is still holding discussions with Fisons, privately admit the possibility that Fisons is just stringing them along, but say that Fisons' powerful legal position makes it dangerous to attack the company openly. One member of the consortium, who asked not to be identified, told me, 'We are afraid to alienate Fisons or to threaten them. They could, and I think they would, rush to destroy the moors. If the ecological interest is gone, they've won. How long would it take them to destroy the moors? A very short time, I suggest.'

Fisons has been taken aback by the onslaught of criticism of its operations on Thorne Moors. 'The attacks came out of the blue,' Egan told me. 'But it's not as though I wasn't aware that we had a conservation responsibility. In fact, *we* were the ones who instigated the conservation interest in Thorne Moors. In 1974, our board endorsed a conservation plan with the Nature Conservancy Council' – for the area that is now the National Nature Reserve. 'The NCC didn't actually buy the land until 1985, if you can believe it, but we were honouring this agreement all that time. . . . If Fisons made one mistake, they didn't educate the people, didn't highlight the conservation work they were doing down the years.' On the other hand, Egan says, it would be easy to overstate the value of Thorne Moors. 'It's of conservation

63

interest, but to a very specialized group of individuals.'

The company now has three public-relations people working full time on conservation issues. And Egan, who was supposed to be managing the Thorne Moors operation, found himself 'spending one and a half to two days a week dealing with conservation issues' – activities that ranged from talking with journalists to negotiating with county planning officials and consulting with the Nature Conservancy Council. 'I feel sad that so much time and effort is being spent in protecting an area that would have been protected anyway,' he told me.

Egan argues that Fisons, and not its environmentalist critics, is the true conservationist, because it, and not the environmentalists, knows how to manage peat bogs. 'None of it is textbook,' he said. 'Each moor is different – each has to be drained in a different way. We are the experts in this field, and we feel we can do a lot for conservation – more than the conservationists. Conservation means management. And management can also mean peat extraction.'

Fisons' plan is to take all but the last eighteen inches of peat and then restore at least part of the moors – the company won't say exactly which part – and leave it as a nature reserve. 'We won't do away with any particular species, or anything like that,' Egan told me. The plan, he said, will encourage regrowth by transferring plants from uncut parts of the moors to areas that the company is finished with. That does not mean transplanting whole sections of turf, I was told this summer by Brian Wheeler.

'Lots of people have tried transplanting turves from one area to another, but, really, the results are not particularly good – basically nothing happens,' he said. Nor will Thorne Moors recover if it is left on its own. Older peat cuttings, there and elsewhere, have regenerated successfully, but bogs that were surface milled as much as thirty years ago have yet to recover, according to Richard Lindsay, the Nature Conservancy Council's peat specialist.

Wheeler is experimenting with a new approach. Working on a twenty-five-acre cut-over site, he is trying to set up the conditions from which Thorne Moors evolved over the past several thousand years, starting with the colonization of open water by cotton grass (several species of sedge that grow in shallow water), in the hope that nature will repeat the process, eventually creating a new raised bog on Thorne Moors. 'But you can't just flood the system as it is,' Wheeler says. 'We think you need to even it out' – into a 'corrugated surface' of ridges and hollows to eliminate 'high and dry' spots. Wheeler estimates that it will be ten to twenty years before he can say how the worked-out peatlands should be landscaped.

Once the experimental plot is landscaped and flooded, cotton grass is to be transplanted there, on the theory that the floating plants will allow sphagnum mosses to colonize the area, and turn Thorne Moors back into a raised peat bog. No one knows how long this might take. Wheeler thinks that there would be 'some good regrowth in fifty to a hundred years', but that the complete evolution to a raised bog, if it does occur, would take much longer.

There is uncertainty about how much peat Fisons would have to leave behind to make the experiment a success. According to David Bellamy, who has done surveys on Thorne Moors for Fisons, 'they've got to leave at least a metre of peat' – roughly forty inches – 'and then they can cut down another half metre' to form the hollows. Brian Wheeler is considering hollows from one to two metres deep – three to six feet. Yet Fisons has often said that it intends to leave just half a metre – slightly under twenty inches – of peat behind when it pulls out. However much peat the company and its scientific advisers finally agree should be left, there is the additional problem that it is difficult to know exactly when that point has been reached, since the peat sits on an uneven layer of clay. In looking at cross-section views afforded by drains dug into the moors, I noticed several areas that appear to have less than half a metre of peat left now. Fisons' own records state that on parts of the illegally cut Snaith and Cowick Moors the company has left less than a fifth of a metre of peat. In a few places on Thorne Moors, Fisons has already taken all the peat, leaving the clay subsurface exposed. The Doncaster and District Ornithological Society reported in 1986 that the peat on Thorne Moors 'is nowhere deeper than about 2.5 metres'.

Wheeler acknowledges that his plan may not work. He is wrestling with an untried technology. The difficulties are myriad: from the mundane problem of how to obtain enough cotton grass to the profound one of whether it is possible to re-create the centuries-long evolution of a habitat without re-creating the environmental conditions (climate, for example) that existed over that period. Of the chances of re-creating a raised peat bog Roger Meade, a peatland specialist and the Nature Conservancy Council's officer responsible for Thorne Moors, says, 'It's speculative.' And Brian Eversham says,'You might be able to grow sphagnum moss, but sphagnum moss doesn't make a peat bog, any more than pine trees make a forest. A peat bog is a community of hundreds of plants and animals, and you can't just grow those.'

A key question is whether the plants and animals left on Thorne Moors after Fisons goes will survive long enough to be able to recolonize a second-generation moor. Company spokesmen point with pride to roughly seven hundred and fifty acres of 'nature reserves' now on the moors, which they say will constitute a refuge for insects, birds, and plants displaced by peat operations. 'In that area, you should be well able to house all the particular species that are of value to the site,' Egan says. Only the hundred-and-eighty-acre National Nature Reserve, which is owned by the Nature Conservancy Council, and a hundred and eighty-five acres of land managed by a local naturalist trust under an agreement with Fisons have legal protection, however. The remainder, less than four hundred acres, consists of small parcels of unprotected land that have already been cut over or contain too little peat to be worth extracting.

Some of these parcels are being used as 'donor' sites for Wheeler's restoration experiment; that is, the vegetation has been scraped off by heavy machinery and taken to the experiment site, so that suitable plants can be transplanted.

There are many species that the total reserves are too small to support in viable numbers, including birds of prey such as merlins and hen harriers, which rely on the moors as a winter habitat, and the northern eggar moth, which requires a square mile of peatland to forage over. Nor are the reserves representative of the full range of habitats on Thorne Moors. Several of the most important habitats on the moors are unprotected and are scheduled for complete elimination within the next five years. 'The raft spider's habitat will disappear from the moors within a year, according to Fisons' cutting plans,' Brian Eversham says. In addition, the reserves, though they are not being drained themselves, are threatened by drainage elsewhere. So far, no way has been discovered to maintain the high water tables they need to survive while the land all around them is being drained.

No peat bog in Britain has been successfully restored, and the experience of peat-restoration projects elsewhere is not encouraging. In the early nineteen-eighties, after spending thirty-three million pounds on an attempt to restore five tiny parcels of bog, at a cost of two million pounds per square metre, Dutch conservationists decided that it made more sense to protect unspoiled bogs. Since all Holland's peat bogs have already been destroyed,

Dutch conservation groups have bought several of Ireland's most severely threatened peat bogs.

Critics may doubt whether Fisons will really pay for such an expensive and uncertain restoration project, but Egan insists that the restoration will happen, because it makes good business sense. 'We see Thorne Moors as being a wetland habitat,' he told me. 'There's not much else we can do with it, and it wouldn't be good for Fisons to walk away leaving a desert landscape behind. It's important to retain a good public image. Besides, everybody wants his little monument, and we'd like to leave behind something we're proud of.' Those who dwell on the difficulties of re-creating a peat bog also exasperate him. 'What are we trying to do?' he said. 'Every eight hundred years, it's been a different landscape. At one time, it was under water. Do we keep it always the way it is now? I mean, a peat bog formed before; it'll form again if conditions are right.'

Whatever the likelihood of Fisons' creating a new peat bog on the site of the one it has destroyed, many ecologists and conservationists are disturbed by the notion that it is all right to destroy an ecosystem if something else can be made to grow in its place later on. 'The fact that eventually something, maybe even some kind of peat bog, will grow again on this site – if the developers are kept off for several centuries – is no excuse for destroying the living community that is there now,' Jane Smart says. Brian Wheeler agrees with this argument – in part, at least. 'I would very strongly resist any attempt to drain a pristine ecosystem on the ground that it could be re-created,' he told me. 'But Fisons is cutting away at a highly damaged raised bog. . . . Much of what is left there is appallingly miserable, a mixture of birch and bracken.'

No ecologist would argue with the contention that Thorne Moors is no longer a pure raised bog. Man's actions there over the centuries have turned parts of it into a fen habitat, with a completely different set of plants and insects from the ones that can survive in the acid parts of the moorland. Other parts have dried out so much that they have been colonized by birch trees and bracken, and these parts have become important breeding and feeding places for some of Britain's rarest and best-loved birds, including nightjars, whinchats, and long-eared owls. This patchwork quality, some ecologists argue, is all the more reason for protecting the moorland. 'Its great diversity and its size are what make Thorne Moors valuable – not just the fact that part of it is a raised bog,' Brian Eversham says. And Jane Smart says, 'You can't look at this thing just as a botanist or just as a peat-bog person. You have to look at the mixture that nature and history have given you, and not set a level of purity and ignore anything that falls short. How we treat our working land, the land that has produced for us, is a better measure of our society and of our future than how we treat the few pristine places we have left.'

The Photographs

Common reeds growing in an abandoned canal on the
National Nature Reserve, which was used to transport peat
by barge in the early 20th century.

Wide drainage ditch showing clay substrate
under the remaining peat.

Cotton grass and a disused drainage channel on the NNR.

Rushes reflected in a drain on the National Nature Reserve.

Tufted hair grass on Crowle Moors.

Vegetation recovering on a dry peat baulk after a major fire.

Rushes and birch growing on old peat workings –
Crowle Moors.

Regenerating birch, Crowle Moors.

Abandoned peat cuttings on the NNR
showing bog pools, sphagnum moss and cotton grass.
Thorne Colliery is in the background.

3,000-year-old tree stumps disturbed during
drainage operations on an area of modern peat extraction –
a site designated as an SSSI.

An SSSI where modern methods of peat extraction
are taking place.

Limestone access road into peat milling fields.

appendix

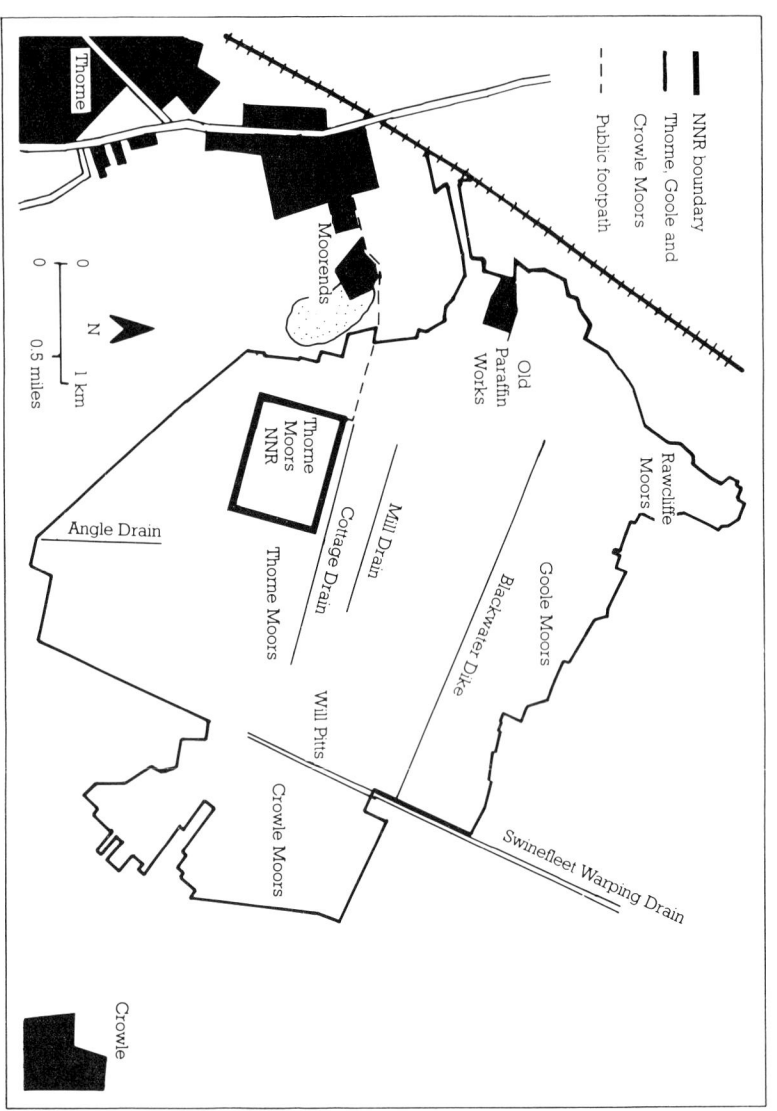

Thorne Moors and surrounding district

Reproduced by kind permission of *English Nature*

Map labels:

NNR boundary

Thorne, Goole and Crowle Moors

Public footpath

Thorne

Moorends

Moorends

Old Paraffin Works

Rawcliffe Moors

Thorne Moors NNR

Angle Drain

Mill Drain

Cottage Drain

Thorne Moors

Blackwater Dike

Goole Moors

Will Pitts

Crowle Moors

Swinefleet Warping Drain

Crowle

N

0   0.5 miles

0   1 km

Thorne Moors National Nature Reserve

Canal 1

New cut drain

Canal 2

Canal 3

Canal 4

Canal 5

Canal 6

Northern Canal

Southern boundary drain

N

0   200
metres

Disused peat cuttings with sphagna/cotton grass communities

Dry peat baulks with birch, bracken and heather

Disused canals with poor fen vegetation

Disused main drainage channels

Drains with open water

Path

Reproduced by kind permission of *English Nature*

Access to Thorne Moors National Nature Reserve is available by permit only, from The Warden, English Nature, 44 Bond Street, Wakefield, West Yorkshire, WF1 2QP.

Access to the remainder of the moors is strictly controlled by Fisons plc, from whom permission must be obtained by contacting Fisons plc, Horticulture Division, Hatfield Peat Works, Thorne, Doncaster DN8 5TE.

Useful addresses:

Plantlife
The Natural History Museum
Cromwell Road
London SW7 5RD
Plantlife is dedicated to the conservation of plants and their habitats throughout Britain, Ireland and abroad.

Friends of the Earth
26-28 Underwood Street
London
N1 75Q
Friends of the Earth are an environmental pressure group. They have produced two guides to peat alternatives.

English Nature Headquarters
Northminster House
Peterborough
PE1 1UA
English Nature, formally the Nature Conservancy Council for England, is the Government's advisor on nature conservation in England.